RAYMOND ARROYO

New York Times bestselling author

THE UNEXPECTED LIGHT OF THOMAS ALVA EDISON

Illustrated by
KRISTINA GEHRMANN

To all the mothers—like Rebecca and Lynda—who see
the promise in their children long before the world does.

—RA

ZONDERKIDZ

The Unexpected Light of Thomas Alva Edison
Copyright © 2023 by Raymond Arroyo
Illustrations © 2023 by Raymond Arroyo

Requests for information should be addressed to:

Zonderkidz, 3900 Sparks Drive, Grand Rapids, Michigan 49546

Hardcover ISBN 978-0-310-79923-8
Ebook ISBN 978-0-310-79924-5

Library of Congress Cataloging-in-Publication Data
Names: Arroyo, Raymond, author. | Gehrmann, Kristina, illustrator.
Title: The unexpected light of Thomas Alva Edison / by Raymond Arroyo.
Description: Grand Rapids : Zonderkidz, [2023] | Audience: Ages 4-8 |
   Summary: "From New York Times bestselling author and news anchor Raymond
   Arroyo comes a picture book biography of one of America's most famous
   inventors, Thomas Alva Edison, and a story about how a small spark can
   create a big light. No one thought much of young Thomas Alva Edison. He
   couldn't focus at school and caused trouble around the house. But where
   others saw a distracted and mischievous boy, his mother saw imagination
   and curiosity. When he was only seven years old, Al, as he was called as
   a young child, got kicked out of school and from then on his mother
   oversaw his rigorous at-home education while also allowing him great
   freedom to explore and dream. Those early years of encouragement and
   loving guidance formed the man who would apply those valuable lessons as
   well as his rich imagination to inventing the phonograph, the motion
   picture camera, the light bulb and more. Inside, readers will: meet the
   larger-than-life personality of Thomas Alva Edison, hear a tale of an
   underdog overcoming all the odds, learn about the power of curiosity,
   and take a carefully researched and actively told romp through
   history"-- Provided by publisher.
Identifiers: LCCN 2022005560 (print) | LCCN 2022005561 (ebook) | ISBN
   9780310799238 (hardcover) | ISBN 9780310799245 (ebook)
Subjects: LCSH: Edison, Thomas A. (Thomas Alva), 1847-1931--Juvenile
   literature. | Edison, Thomas A. (Thomas Alva), 1847-1931--Childhood and
   youth--Juvenile literature. | Inventors--United States--Juvenile
   literature. | Mothers and sons--Juvenile literature.
Classification: LCC TK140.E3 A77 2023 (print) | LCC TK140.E3 (ebook) |
   DDC 621.3092 [B]--dc23/eng/20220909
LC record available at https://lccn.loc.gov/2022005560
LC ebook record available at https://lccn.loc.gov/2022005561

Illustrations: Kristina Gehrmann
Editor: Katherine Jacobs
Design and art direction: Cindy Davis

Printed in Italy

23 24 25 26 27 28 / RTLO / 21 20 19 18 17 16 15 14 13 12 11 10 9 8 7 6 5 4 3 2 1

As a baby, little Al Edison slept in a dark, windowless attic. But there was light within him.

Al was forever getting into trouble, which sometimes happens when you're curious.

He was interested in everything from how birds flew to where bees lived to how steamboats moved along the big canals behind his house.

Whenever his mother wasn't watching, he snuck down to the waterway for a closer look.

Sometimes he got a bit too close!

But most of all, Al wanted to know how things worked.
He explored the town, noticing everything, and he sketched
whatever drew his attention, like the shop signs in the town square.

Once, when he wondered how a grain elevator carried grain up into its storage bins, he climbed inside, and found out for himself.

At home, Al peppered his parents with questions: "Who?" "What?" "Why?" "How?"

After a while his father had enough.

"I don't know!" he yelled.

"Why don't you know?" Al asked.

His mother patiently answered his questions.

8

When Al asked, "Why does the goose squat on the eggs?" she said, "To keep them warm."

"Why does she keep them warm?"

"To hatch them, my dear."

Al's eyes widened. "Keeping the eggs warm makes the little geese come out?"

"Yes."

Al had an idea.

His father found him hours later in a neighbor's barn, lying on top of a big nest filled with goose and chicken eggs. This might have been Thomas Alva Edison's first experiment. He didn't hatch any geese, but he did manage to outrage his father.

Later, when Al was six years old, his curiosity about fire got the best of him. He set a small blaze in his father's barn "just to see what it would do."

The blaze torched the entire building and the flames nearly spread across town. His furious dad punished him in the public square. As painful as it was, it did nothing to stifle Al's curiosity.

Against his father's wishes, Al would sometimes run along the canal to the workshop of a man called "the Mad Miller of Milan." Sam Winchester, a flour mill owner, was trying to create a balloon big enough to carry people into the sky. He even burned down his own mill during one of the experiments—which fascinated Al.

He would press his face against the workshop window as the miller tinkered and fiddled with the hydrogen needed to lift his balloon. If one approach didn't work, the miller would try something else. The intensity of those experiments showed young Al that hands-on hard work could unlock amazing discoveries.

When he was seven years old, Al's family moved to Port Huron, Michigan. There, he was enrolled in Reverend G.B. Engle's one-room schoolhouse. Gone were the trips to the canal and the daring, hands-on experiments. During the boring lectures, Al fidgeted, daydreamed, and didn't respond to questions at all.

He's "addled," the schoolmaster announced publicly, convinced that Al Edison couldn't be taught. A heartbroken Al ran home to his mother in tears.

14

The next day, Mrs. Edison stormed into the school with her son in tow. She told Reverend Engle that he "didn't know what he was talking about." She had seen the light in her son and knew he "had more brains than" even the teacher himself. From that day on, she told the schoolmaster, she would educate Al at home.

Mrs. Edison introduced Al to Shakespeare and Charles Dickens. He read *A School Compendium of Natural and Experimental Philosophy*, from cover to cover. The book explained electricity, mechanics, and the electric telegraph.

Al was so intrigued that he sketched and then built his own telegraph line to a neighbor's house.

Chemistry books inspired ten-year-old Al to build a lab at home.
To protect her furniture, his mother relocated it to the family cellar.

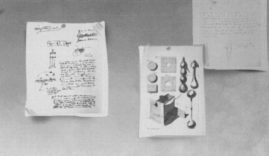

Downstairs, his attempts to create a battery with jars of acid caused the occasional explosion.

"He will blow us all up," his father fumed.

"Let him be," his mother said. "Al knows what he's about."

Money was always tight for the Edisons. So at twelve years old, Al convinced his parents to allow him to sell newspapers, candy, and food aboard the new Grand Trunk Railway, a train line that ran between Port Huron and Detroit.

The clatter and squeal of the train barely phased Al. This was when he began to realize he had lost most of his hearing.

But deafness proved a gift for young Edison. "In my isolation, I had time to think things out," he later said. "Deafness probably drove me to reading." During the six and half hour layover in Detroit each day, Al could be found at the public library. He began with the books on the lowest shelves of the library, and read his way to the top shelves in no time.

To put his ever-growing knowledge to use, Al got permission from the conductor to set up a mobile laboratory in the train's baggage car.

His experiments continued until a collision caused some chemicals to spill, setting the baggage compartment on fire.

Unstoppable, Al used recycled metal type and an old handpress to print his own newspaper in the train's baggage car. The *Weekly Herald* was filled with death notices, local stories, and gossip. The paper lasted until a man, upset by something Al had printed, threw him into the St. Clair River.

One afternoon, at the Mount Clemens station, Al was selling papers on the platform while his train changed cars. Suddenly a boxcar broke free and rolled toward a three year old child playing on the tracks. Al dropped his papers, leapt off the platform, and scooped up the child, saving his life.

The child's father, James Mckenzie, was the station telegrapher. To thank Al for saving his son, Mckenzie offered to teach Edison how to use the telegraph.

Al remembered the homemade telegraph line he had strung to his neighbor's house and imagined himself tapping out dashes and dots on a real machine, sending messages for much longer distances. He accepted the offer.

By the time he was sixteen years old, Al dropped his nickname and began using his first name, Tom. He was now a real plug telegrapher. But tapping a metal key to send messages across the country wasn't enough to satisfy Tom's curiosity.

He had ideas about how the power of electricity could improve daily life. So he created his first invention: an automatic voting machine. He tried to sell it to congress, but they weren't interested.

Then came a blow Tom never expected: He received a telegram that his mother had died. He rushed home for the funeral of the first person who believed in him—the one who kindled the light of his curiosity.

To honor his mother, and to prove himself worthy of her confidence, he threw himself into his work. In 1876, Tom opened what he called "the invention factory" in Menlo Park, New Jersey. Here, he and his "muckers" —a team of curious inventors and experimenters—turned dreams into reality.

Chock-full of inventions and inspirations, Tom would experiment through the night, taking short naps on the lab's workbenches. He threw himself over tables, furiously scrawling ideas in his notebooks.

What kind of device could record sound?

How would one capture moving images?

Which material could conduct enough electricity to extend the glow of a light bulb?

The current of ingenuity surged through him.

And inventions flowed out of Tom.

Thomas Alva Edison filled more than 3,000 notebooks with design sketches. He created the light bulb, the phonograph to record music, the motion picture camera, and so much more.

Springing from those jars of acid he mixed in his mother's basement so many years earlier, he invented the alkaline storage battery. But the light of invention within Tom might never have illuminated the world, had it not been for a mother who first saw the glow of curiosity in her Al.

Author's Note

It was Edison's comment late in life about his mother that drew me to his story and became the heart of this Turnabout Tale. The great inventor said: "My mother was the making of me … I did not have my mother for very long but in that length of time she cast over me an influence which has lasted all my life. The good effects of her early training I can never lose. If it had not been for her appreciation and her faith in me at a critical time in my experience, I should very likely never had become an inventor."

We often forget that talent is nurtured and revealed by love and belief. Nancy Edison, a former schoolteacher in Canada, understood the inherent spark in her boy and his unique gifts. She was tough on him, making him study while the other boys played. Edison said his mother taught him how to "read good books quickly and correctly." She is perhaps the most important and overlooked aspect of the Edison story.

Not only did his mother give him the confidence to pursue his passions and gather knowledge, but both his parents were hard workers. Thomas Edison carried that work ethic into adulthood. Forsaking sleep, meals, and time off, he practically lived in his lab. His was a process of excited, hands-on experimentation, marked by much trial and error. Edison's childlike curiosity never dimmed. There are stories of him hurling himself over worktables to see experiments close up and madly recording his observations in notebooks. The great inventor would often, by his own admission, pick up where the last inventor left off. He was a lifelong problem solver who pushed for solutions where others had given up. During his 84 years, Edison secured 1,093 patents, not only lighting up cities but revolutionizing the lives of people around the world. Edison's inventions from the phonograph to the first electric car not only enlightened his age, but our own. "Every wrong attempt discarded is another step forward," he said. "Sticking to it is the genius."

That approach applies not only to inventions, but to people as well. As Nancy Edison attests: The genius is sometimes found by sticking to them—and by them.

Further Reading and Bibliography

Adkins, Jan, *Thomas Edison*; New York, DK Publishing, 2009.

Baldwin, Neil, *Edison Inventing the Century*; New York, Hyperion, 1995.

Delano, Marfe' Ferguson; *Inventing the Future, The Photography of Thomas Alva Edison*; Washington, DC, National Geographic, 2002.

Josephson, Matthew, *Edison*; New York, McGraw-Hill, 1959.

Rutgers University Thomas Edison Papers Collection: edison.rutgers.edu/